Content

Written by
Dee Reid

Illustrated by
Dylan Gibson

Series editor **Dee Reid**

Heinemann

Part of Pearson

Characters

Imran

Tariq

Mr Ali

Tariq's Aunty

Tricky words

- thought
- teabags
- basket

- really
- someone
- everyone

Read these words to the student. Help them with these words when they appear in the text.

Introduction

Tariq is in the year above Imran at school. Sometimes they get on OK but sometimes Tariq likes to boss Imran around. One day Imran was in the shop getting some things for his mum. On the list was pink loo paper.

SHAMED

teabags
milk
pink loo roll
eggs
crisps
bread

Imran was in the shop.
He had a list of things to get.

I hate shopping, thought Imran. But mum will be cross if I don't get the things on the list.

4

Imran put teabags in the basket.
I hope no-one from school sees me,
he thought.

Mum had put 'pink loo paper' on the list but Imran couldn't see pink loo paper. *I really hate shopping*, thought Imran.

Imran asked Mr Ali about pink loo paper.
I hope no-one from school hears me,
thought Imran.

Mr Ali gave Imran the pink loo paper.
Imran put it in the basket.

I really hope no-one from school sees me, thought Imran.

"Nice loo paper," said someone.
It was Tariq.
"I will tell everyone in school about the pink loo paper," said Tariq.

"Tariq, darling, give Aunty a kiss," said someone and a big lady gave Tariq a kiss.

"If you tell everyone in school about the pink loo paper, I will get you!" said Imran.

"If you tell everyone in school about the kiss, I will get you," said Tariq.

Quiz /////////////////////////

Text comprehension

Literal comprehension
p4 Did Imran like shopping for his mum?
p10 How does Tariq plan to embarrass Imran?

Inferential comprehension
p7 Why did Imran hope no-one from school would hear him?
p11 How is Tariq embarrassed?
p12 How does Imran make sure Tariq won't tell about the pink loo paper?

Personal response
• Would you feel embarrassed if a mate saw you buying loo paper?
• Has a member of your family ever embarrassed you? How?

Word knowledge

p4 Which two words are contracted in 'don't'?
p5 Find a compound word.
p11 What words did Tariq's Aunty say?

Spelling challenge

Read these words: **will   you   don't**
Now try to spell them!

Ha! Ha! Ha!

Why did the traffic light turn red?

You would too if you had to change in the middle of the street!

Find out about

- people who go on talent shows because they want to be a star.

Tricky words

- talent
- rubbish
- watching
- embarrassing
- ice skating
- wrong

Read these words to the student. Help them with these words when they appear in the text.

Introduction

Lots of people go on talent shows because they want to show they are good at something. But sometimes things go wrong and they can embarrass themselves. How would you feel if you were on a talent show and it all went wrong?

How Embarrassing!

Lots of people like to go
on talent shows.
They want to show they
are good at something.
They want to be a star.

Some people on talent shows
are good but lots of people
are no good at all.
They are rubbish!

Sometimes on talent shows
people do things that go wrong
when everyone is watching them.
How embarrassing is that?

This man was on a talent show.
He wanted to show he was good at
ice skating but he was no good at all!
He was rubbish at ice skating!
He skated off the ice!

How would you feel if you did something wrong when everyone was watching you?

This woman was on a talent show.
She wanted to show how good
she was at singing.
She wanted to be a star but
she did not look like a star.
Would she embarrass herself?

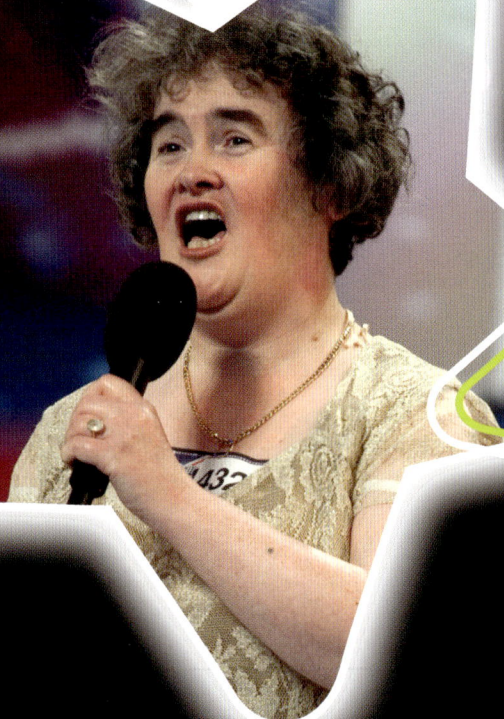

Then she started singing.
She was good!
She did not embarrass herself.
She was a star!

Are you good at something?
Would you go on a talent show?
What if you did something
embarrassing?

Quiz //////////////////////////

Text comprehension

Literal comprehension
p15 Why do people go on talent shows?
p18 What embarrassing things can happen on talent shows?

Inferential comprehension
p19 How might people feel if things go wrong when they are on a talent show?
p20 Why might the audience think some people won't be any good?
p20 Does the audience always want the person to be a star?

Personal response
• Why do you think talent shows are so popular on TV?
• Is it OK to laugh at someone who makes a mistake on a talent show?

Word knowledge

p17 Find a word that means the opposite of 'right'.
p18 Why are there three exclamation marks on this page?
p19 Find a compound word.

Spelling challenge

Read these words:
how   this   good
Now try to spell them!

Ha! Ha! Ha!

What do you get if you cross an iPod with a fridge?

Cool music!